Leonardo da Vinci
1452-1519

Leonardo da Vinci (1452-1519) was born in Italy, the son of a gentleman of Florence. He made significant contributions to many different disciplines, including anatomy, botany, geology, astronomy, architecture, paleontology, and cartography.

He is one of the greatest and most influential painters of all time, creating masterpieces such as the *Mona Lisa* and *The Last Supper*. And his imagination led him to create designs for things such as an armored car, scuba gear, a parachute, a revolving bridge, and flying machines. Many of these ideas were so far ahead of their time that they weren't built until centuries later.

He is the original "Renaissance Man" whose genius extended to all five areas of today's STEAM curriculum: Science, Technology, Engineering, the Arts, and Mathematics.

You can find more information on Leonardo da Vinci in *Who Was Leonardo da Vinci?* by Roberta Edwards (Grosset & Dunlap, 2005), *Magic Tree House Fact Tracker: Leonardo da Vinci* by Mary Pope Osborne and Natalie Pope Bryce (Random House, 2009), and *Leonardo da Vinci for Kids: His Life and Ideas* by Janis Herbert (Chicago Review Press, 1998).

Little Leonardo's™

Fascinating World

of ASTRONOMY

Illustrated by
GREG PAPROCKI

Written by
SARAFINA NANCE

GIBBS SMITH
TO ENRICH AND INSPIRE HUMANKIND

ASTRONOMY is the science of studying the Universe. The UNIVERSE is full of things we can see, such as planets, moons, and stars, and things we can't see, such as dark matter and dark energy.

Everything you can see, touch, taste, and smell is actually just a teeny tiny part of the Universe. The rest of the Universe is made up of invisible matter, called DARK MATTER, and a mysterious force making the Universe get bigger and bigger over time, called DARK ENERGY!

Composition of the Universe

- 68% Dark Energy ???
- 27% Dark Matter ??
- 5% Normal Matter

Of the matter we can see, some of the brightest are stars. A STAR is an extremely hot ball of gas. Our nearest star is the Sun!

Our Sun, like all living stars, shines with **LIGHT**. Sunlight allows the Earth to brighten during the day, and the hot temperatures from the Sun heat up our summers. Sunlight is even responsible for our sunburns!

Deep inside the star, within the STELLAR CORE, tiny particles called ELEMENTS slam into each other to create light. This light, or starshine, is proof that some stars are alive.

STELLAR CORE

ELEMENTS

At the ends of their lives, stars can't shine any longer. Stars like our Sun fizzle out and fade away, shrinking to become WHITE DWARFS. And bigger stars explode as SUPERNOVAE. Some explosions leave behind a NEUTRON STAR, others collapse into BLACK HOLES, and the rest explode entirely, leaving nothing behind.

WHITE DWARFS

SUPERNOVA

NEUTRON STAR

BLACK HOLE

PLANETS orbit stars, making up cosmic neighborhoods called SOLAR SYSTEMS. In our solar system we have eight planets, all of which ORBIT the Sun. These eight planets are called Mercury, Venus, Earth, Mars, Jupiter, Saturn, Uranus, and Neptune.

Earth is our home planet. It is made of saltwater oceans, freshwater lakes and rivers, polar ice caps, and land. It is the only planet known to HARBOR life, making it a special home for us!

The Earth has one MOON, which orbits Earth and is thought to have formed through the BIG SPLASH. The Big Splash occurred when the Earth was just forming and a nearby small planet crashed into it. Our Moon is thought to have formed from the mixture created when the two planets combined.

Although our planet only has 1 Moon, Jupiter has 79 and Saturn has 82 moons!

Some planets are made of gas, like Jupiter, and some are made of rock, like Earth. Some planets, such as 55 CANCRI E, are even made of diamond!

Planets that orbit stars other than the Sun are called **EXOPLANETS**. There are thousands of other planets in our home galaxy, which is called the **MILKY WAY**.

Some planets are as small as the Moon, and others are even bigger than Jupiter, the largest planet in our solar system. Jupiter is so big that 1,300 Earths could fit inside of it!

Many, many solar systems made up of planets and stars form GALAXIES. Unlike our solar system, which only has one star, some solar systems have two stars. These are called BINARY SYSTEMS.

At the center of our galaxy is a supermassive black hole called **SAGITTARIUS A***, around which all of the stars and planets in the galaxy orbit.

Humans learn all about the objects in the night sky by using **TELESCOPES**. The main job of a telescope is to collect light. The bigger the telescope is, the more light it collects and the farther away it can see. The biggest telescopes can spot the most distant objects in our Universe, such as the first-ever galaxies and stars.

Light comes in many different forms.
In fact, human eyes are only able to see a small portion
of all the light in the Universe.

The rest of the light in the Universe is invisible to the human eye, in the form of low-energy RADIO WAVES, medium-energy ULTRAVIOLET WAVES, and high-energy GAMMA RAYS. Microwaves, televisions, and X-ray machines all use these types of invisible light to work!

Telescopes are built to detect all forms of light, including those that our eyes can't see. There are telescopes in valleys, on mountaintops, and even in space! Depending on where a telescope sits, it can detect different types of light.

Studying the Universe allows humans to study important questions such as:

Where did the Universe come from?

How will the Universe end?

Is there other life out there?

What questions will you ask about our Universe?

GLOSSARY

55 CANCRI E: A planet made of diamond orbiting a star like the Sun.

ASTRONOMY: The field of science that uses math, physics, and other sciences to study objects and phenomena outside of the Earth's atmosphere.

BIG SPLASH: A theory for the formation of our Moon, which suggests that the Moon formed from the collision of a  small planet with the Earth.

BINARY SYSTEMS: A system formed when two objects in space, such as stars, orbit each other.

BLACK HOLES: Formed when massive stars explode, and their leftover cores collapse into a tiny region of space.

DARK ENERGY: The mysterious, invisible force propelling the Universe to grow and expand.

DARK MATTER: The invisible matter that makes up 27% of the contents of the Universe.

ELEMENTS: Tiny particles that are the building blocks of all matter in the Universe.

EXOPLANETS: Planets outside of our solar system that orbit stars other than the Sun.

GALAXIES: Groups of stars, gas, dust, and moons that are bound by gravity and move together in the Universe.

GAMMA RAYS: The light in our Universe with the most energy.

HARBOR: To support the growth of something. To give shelter and become a refuge.

LIGHT: A type of energy created in the cores of stars, which exists in small particles called photons.

MILKY WAY: A wide irregular band of light that stretches completely around the celestial sphere. Also our home galaxy.

MOON: A small planet-like object that orbits the Earth.

ASTRONOMY

NEUTRON STAR: The leftover cores of dead stars that explode as supernovae.

ORBIT: The motion of objects traveling around another object, held together by gravity.

PLANETS: Large objects that orbit around stars.

RADIO WAVES: Light in our Universe that is used for radio telecommunications.

SAGITTARIUS A*: The supermassive black hole at the center of the Milky Way, which holds our galaxy together.

SOLAR SYSTEMS: Systems of stars and orbiting planets.

STAR: A celestial object made up of gas and energy that shines when alive.

STELLAR CORE: The innermost part of a star, where light is created.

SUPERNOVAE: An explosion of a massive star when it is at the end of its life.

TELESCOPES: The primary tool that astronomers use to study the Universe. Telescopes collect light, allowing astronomers to see distant objects.

ULTRAVIOLET WAVES: Light in our Universe that is responsible for sunburns.

UNIVERSE: Everything we can touch, taste, see, smell, measure, and explore, for all time.

WHITE DWARFS: The leftover cores of dead stars that are not massive enough to explode as supernovae or collapse into black holes.

Manufactured in China in June 2021 by Crash Paper

First Edition
25 24 23 22 21   5 4 3 2 1

Published by
Gibbs Smith
P.O. Box 667
Layton, Utah 84041
1.800.835.4993 orders
www.gibbs-smith.com

Designed by Greg Paprocki

Gibbs Smith books are printed on either recycled,
100% post-consumer waste, FSC-certified papers or on
paper produced from sustainable PEFC-certified forest/
controlled wood source. Learn more at www.pefc.org.

Library of Congress Control Number: 2021931693
ISBN: 978-1-4236-5831-3

Some astronomers of note . . .

Benjamin Banneker (1731-1806)

A free man during a time when many African Americans were slaves, he taught himself calculations
to predict the motions of the Moon and other planets and wrote a series of almanacs. At the age
of 54, he even predicted an eclipse! He advocated for the end of slavery, and he and President
Thomas Jefferson exchanged letters tackling racial equality.

Subrahmanyan Chandrasekhar (1910-1995)

Subrahmanyan was an Indian-American astrophysicist who, at the age of 19, began his work that
led to a Nobel Prize in Physics in 1983 for discovering that many massive stars collapse under
their own gravity. These collapsed stars form black holes and neutron stars. Chandrasekhar also
attempted to cultivate the mathematical theory of black holes, writing the still-famous book *The
Mathematical Theory of Black Holes*.

Henrietta Swan Leavitt (1868-1921)

Henrietta worked as a "computer" at the Harvard College Observatory where she calculated and
analyzed photos of over 100 areas of the night sky. She transformed astronomy by finding extremely
far-away stars, and her work formed the basis of the discovery that the Universe is expanding.

Vera Rubin (1928-2016)

Vera was an American astronomer who discovered the invisible "missing matter" within galaxies
that we now call dark matter. She was the first woman invited to use the Palomar telescope, and
her observations from this telescope helped her to specialize in how galaxies rotate. Her activism
helped to open science to more women.

Jedidah Isler (unknown-)

Jedidah is an African-American astrophysicist, educator, and active advocate for diversity in
STEM fields. She researches blazars, or hyperactive supermassive black holes, and studies the j
streams shooting out from them. In 2014, she was the first African-American woman to receive
her PhD in Astrophysics from Yale University.

NEUTRON STAR: The leftover cores of dead stars that explode as supernovae.

ORBIT: The motion of objects traveling around another object, held together by gravity.

PLANETS: Large objects that orbit around stars.

RADIO WAVES: Light in our Universe that is used for radio telecommunications.

SAGITTARIUS A*: The supermassive black hole at the center of the Milky Way, which holds our galaxy together.

SOLAR SYSTEMS: Systems of stars and orbiting planets.

STAR: A celestial object made up of gas and energy that shines when alive.

STELLAR CORE: The innermost part of a star, where light is created.

SUPERNOVAE: An explosion of a massive star when it is at the end of its life.

TELESCOPES: The primary tool that astronomers use to study the Universe. Telescopes collect light, allowing astronomers to see distant objects.

ULTRAVIOLET WAVES: Light in our Universe that is responsible for sunburns.

UNIVERSE: Everything we can touch, taste, see, smell, measure, and explore, for all time.

WHITE DWARFS: The leftover cores of dead stars that are not massive enough to explode as supernovae or collapse into black holes.

Manufactured in China in June 2021 by Crash Paper

First Edition
25 24 23 22 21   5 4 3 2 1

Published by
Gibbs Smith
P.O. Box 667
Layton, Utah 84041
1.800.835.4993 orders
www.gibbs-smith.com

Designed by Greg Paprocki

Gibbs Smith books are printed on either recycled,
100% post-consumer waste, FSC-certified papers or on
paper produced from sustainable PEFC-certified forest/
controlled wood source. Learn more at www.pefc.org.

Library of Congress Control Number: 2021931693
ISBN: 978-1-4236-5831-3

Some astronomers of note . . .

Benjamin Banneker (1731–1806)

A free man during a time when many African Americans were slaves, he taught himself calculations to predict the motions of the Moon and other planets and wrote a series of almanacs. At the age of 54, he even predicted an eclipse! He advocated for the end of slavery, and he and President Thomas Jefferson exchanged letters tackling racial equality.

Subrahmanyan Chandrasekhar (1910–1995)

Subrahmanyan was an Indian-American astrophysicist who, at the age of 19, began his work that led to a Nobel Prize in Physics in 1983 for discovering that many massive stars collapse under their own gravity. These collapsed stars form black holes and neutron stars. Chandrasekhar also attempted to cultivate the mathematical theory of black holes, writing the still-famous book *The Mathematical Theory of Black Holes.*

Henrietta Swan Leavitt (1868–1921)

Henrietta worked as a "computer" at the Harvard College Observatory where she calculated and analyzed photos of over 100 areas of the night sky. She transformed astronomy by finding extremely far-away stars, and her work formed the basis of the discovery that the Universe is expanding.

Vera Rubin (1928–2016)

Vera was an American astronomer who discovered the invisible "missing matter" within galaxies that we now call dark matter. She was the first woman invited to use the Palomar telescope, and her observations from this telescope helped her to specialize in how galaxies rotate. Her activism helped to open science to more women.

Jedidah Isler (unknown–)

Jedidah is an African-American astrophysicist, educator, and active advocate for diversity in STEM fields. She researches blazars, or hyperactive supermassive black holes, and studies the jet streams shooting out from them. In 2014, she was the first African-American woman to receive her PhD in Astrophysics from Yale University.

ASTRONOMY